Use of English

Another ten practice tests for
the Cambridge C1 Advanced

PROSPERITY EDUCATION
www.prosperityeducation.net

Registered offices: Sherlock Close, Cambridge
CB3 0HP, United Kingdom

First published 2023

ISBN: 978-1-915654-08-3

Cover design and typesetting by ORP Cambridge

For further information and resources, visit:
www.prosperityeducation.net

To infinity and beyond.

Contents

Introduction

Welcome to this third edition of sample tests for the Cambridge C1 Advanced (CAE), Use of English examination (Parts 1–4).

The pass threshold of the Cambridge C1 Advanced (CAE) is 60%, and so, in order to allow ample time for the Reading parts (Parts 5–8) of Paper 1, it is advisable that candidates complete The Use of English section (Parts 1–4) as quickly as possible while maintaining accuracy. For instance, completing each part in fewer than five minutes will allow 55 minutes in which to complete the Reading parts.

This resource comprises ten whole Use of English tests, answer keys, write-in answer sheets and a marking scheme, allowing you to score each test out of 36 marks.

The content has been written to closely replicate the Cambridge exam experience, and has undergone comprehensive expert and peer review. You or your students, if you are a teacher, will hopefully enjoy the wide range of essay topics and benefit from the repetitive practice, something that is key to preparing for this part of the C1 Advanced (CAE) examination.

We hope that you will find this resource a useful study aid, and we wish you all the best in preparing for the exam.

Prosperity Education
Cambridge, 2023

For more Cambridge exam-preparation materials, including free sample tests and online resources, visit www.prosperityeducation.net

About the C1 Advanced exam

The Use of English section of the C1 Advanced examination is broken down into four parts:

Part 1. Multiple choice cloze	
What is being tested?	This part of the exam mostly tests vocabulary, idioms, collocations, shades of meaning, phrasal verbs, complementation, semantic precision and fixed phrases.
How does it work?	It contains a test with eight gaps, each gap prompting multiple-choice questions. Each question has four possible answers, only one of which is correct.
How is it marked?	One mark is awarded for each correct answer.

Part 2. Open cloze	
What is being tested?	This part of the exam has a lexico-grammatical focus, testing candidates' awareness and control of grammar, fixed phrasing, collocation, semantic precision and, to an extent, vocabulary (the particles/prepositions for phrasal verbs).
How does it work?	It contains a text with eight gaps, each gap representing a missing word. No hints are given: candidates must think of the correct word for each gap.
How is it marked?	One mark is awarded for each correct answer.

Part 3. Word formation	
What is being tested?	This part of the exam focuses on affixation, internal changes and compounding in word formation, and vocabulary.
How does it work?	It contains a text with eight gaps, each gap representing a missing word. Beside each gap is a 'prompt' word that must be altered in some way to complete the sentence correctly.
How is it marked?	One mark is awarded for each correct answer.

Part 4. Key word transformation	
What is being tested?	This part of the exam has a lexico-grammatical focus, testing lexis, grammar and vocabulary.
How does it work?	It contains six sentences, each followed by a 'key' word and an alternative sentence conveying the same meaning as the first but with a gap in the middle. Candidates are to use the keyword provided to complete the second sentence so that it has a similar meaning to the first sentence. Candidates cannot change the keyword provided.
How is it marked?	Each correct answer is broken down into two marks.

Cambridge C1 Advanced Use of English

Test 1

Part 1

For questions 1–8, read the text below and decide which answer best fits each gap. In the separate answer sheet, mark the appropriate answer (A, B, C or D).

Protecting Machu Picchu

Machu Picchu, the iconic Incan citadel located in the Andes Mountains of Peru, is one of the world's most popular tourist destinations. However, the site is currently **(1)**_____ serious challenges from over-exploitation.

The increase in tourism to Machu Picchu has led to overcrowding, which has a negative impact on the site's infrastructure and surrounding environment. Foot **(2)**_____ and visitors' activities have caused damage to the stonework, and erosion has resulted in the loss of soil and vegetation. Moreover, the high volume of tourists also generates a significant amount of waste, which puts a **(3)**_____ on the site's waste-management facilities.

To **(4)**_____ these problems, the Peruvian government has implemented measures to protect the UNESCO World Heritage Site. One of the most significant actions was the establishment of a daily visitor limit, reducing the number of people allowed to enter Machu Picchu from 5,000 to 2,500 per day. This has helped bring **(5)**_____ overcrowding and minimise the impact on the site's infrastructure and environment.

Additionally, visitors are required to follow specific routes and stay within designated areas, and park rangers monitor visitors' activities to ensure compliance. The government has also implemented waste-management programmes, such as recycling and composting, to minimise the environmental **(6)**_____ of tourism.

While these measures have been effective in protecting Machu Picchu, additional **(7)**_____ are needed to ensure the site's long-term sustainability. The government is continuing to work on strategies to manage tourism sustainably, such as promoting responsible tourism practices and investing in further infrastructure improvements. Only **(8)**_____ collective efforts can we ensure that Machu Picchu remains a magnificent destination for future generations to enjoy.

1	A	opposing	B	facing	C	dealing	D	managing
2	A	circulation	B	movement	C	activity	D	traffic
3	A	strain	B	tension	C	force	D	trauma
4	A	address	B	direct	C	attack	D	converse
5	A	out	B	down	C	on	D	about
6	A	shock	B	influence	C	impact	D	power
7	A	calls	B	efforts	C	struggles	D	energies
8	A	through	B	in	C	of	D	above

Part 2

For questions 9–16, read the text below and decide which word best fits each gap. Use only one word for each gap. In the separate answer sheet, write your answers in capital letters, using one box per letter.

Making and breaking habits

Making changes to our habits can pose a formidable challenge, yet even small adjustments can wield a significant impact **(9)**_____ our lives. By adding or eliminating just one thing for 30 days, we can establish fresh patterns of behaviour that can **(10)**_____ to lasting improvements.

For instance, if you aspire to elevate your physical well-being, cutting **(11)**_____ sugar from your diet for 30 days can be a game-changer. This might require forgoing desserts or sugary beverages, but the benefits can **(12)**_____ truly worthwhile. Not only will you feel better, but you may also notice improvements in your skin, energy levels and overall sense of vitality.

Conversely, adding a habit can **(13)**_____ be transformative. For instance, if you want to be more productive, adding a daily meditation practice can help you bolster focus and reduce stress. **(14)**_____ might involve simply finding a quiet place to sit and introspect for a few minutes each day, but the rewards can be significant. You may detect a heightened sense of concentration and invigoration throughout the day, producing a greater sense of calm and clarity.

As **(15)**_____ old saying goes, 'Rome wasn't built in a day'. Making lasting changes to our habits takes time and effort, but by focusing on just one thing for 30 days, we can establish a new, healthier routine. So why not give it a try? Take the first **(16)**_____ towards a healthier, happier you by adding or eliminating just one thing for the next 30 days.

Part 3

For questions 17–24, use the stem word on the right to form the correct word that fills each gap. In the separate answer sheet, write your answers in capital letters, using one box per letter.

Building a sustainable modern school

The SMET School's upcoming project of constructing a new school in Madrid in 2024 presents an opportunity to build an eco-friendly infrastructure. Constructing a building that is environmentally sustainable will require careful consideration and **(17)**_____ planning. **STRATEGY**

One crucial factor to consider is the selection of building materials. Opting for natural, **(18)**_____ and recyclable materials, such as wood, bamboo and steel, can reduce the carbon footprint of the construction project. Additionally, incorporating recycled materials, such as reclaimed wood or recycled glass, can **(19)**_____ reduce the project's environmental impact. **RENEW** **FAR**

Another vital aspect is ensuring the efficient use of energy. Incorporating energy-efficient technology, such as solar panels and geothermal heating and cooling systems, can significantly reduce energy **(20)**_____ and the new school's carbon footprint. The use of energy-efficient lighting and HVAC systems also has the **(21)**_____ to contribute to a more sustainable structure. **CONSUME** **ABLE**

Water conservation is another essential component in **(22)**_____ an eco-friendly infrastructure. Using low-flow toilets and faucets, collecting rainwater for irrigation and implementing landscaping that requires less water can all contribute to water-conservation efforts. **BUILD**

In conclusion, forming an environmentally sustainable infrastructure requires **(23)**_____ consideration and planning. By selecting sustainable construction materials, incorporating energy-efficient technology and implementing water-conservation measures, the SMET School can construct a new building in Madrid that is both **(24)** _____ and eco-friendly. **CARE** **FUNCTION**

Part 4

For questions 25–30, complete the second sentence, using the word given, so that it has a similar meaning to the first sentence. Do not change the word provided and use between three and six words in total. In the separate answer sheet, write your answers in capital letters, using one box per letter.

25 If you need any help, please don't hesitate to ask.

ASSISTANCE

If I can _____ please don't hesitate to ask.

26 I reckon Samantha will become a famous tennis player.

MATTER

It's only _____ until Samantha becomes a famous tennis player.

27 You must never open this door.

ACCOUNT

_____ should this door ever be opened.

28 What used to be my primary school is now a gym.

TURNED

My old primary school _____ a gym.

29 Chide gets on well with his mother-in-law.

TERMS

Chide is _____ with his mother-in-law.

30 A text message told us he was withdrawing from the process.

PULLING

We were told he was _____ text message.

Answer sheet: Cambridge C1 Advanced
Use of English

Test No.

Mark out of 36

Name _____   **Date** _____

Part 1: Multiple choice

8 marks

Mark the appropriate answer (A, B, C or D).

0	A	B	C	D

1	A	B	C	D		5	A	B	C	D
2	A	B	C	D		6	A	B	C	D
3	A	B	C	D		7	A	B	C	D
4	A	B	C	D		8	A	B	C	D

Part 2: Open cloze

8 marks

Write your answers in capital letters, using one box per letter.

0	B	E	C	A	U	S	E				

9											
10											
11											
12											
13											
14											
15											
16											

Part 3: Word formation

Write your answers in capital letters, using one box per letter.

17 ☐☐☐☐☐☐☐☐☐☐☐

18 ☐☐☐☐☐☐☐☐☐☐

19 ☐☐☐☐☐☐☐☐☐☐☐

20 ☐☐☐☐☐☐☐☐☐☐☐

21 ☐☐☐☐☐☐☐☐☐☐☐

22 ☐☐☐☐☐☐☐☐☐☐☐

23 ☐☐☐☐☐☐☐☐☐☐

24 ☐☐☐☐☐☐☐☐☐☐

Part 4: Key word transformation

Write your answers in capital letters, using one box per letter.

25 ☐☐☐☐☐☐☐☐☐☐☐☐☐☐☐☐☐
☐☐☐☐☐☐☐☐☐☐☐☐☐☐☐☐

26 ☐☐☐☐☐☐☐☐☐☐☐☐☐☐☐☐☐
☐☐☐☐☐☐☐☐☐☐☐☐☐☐☐☐

27 ☐☐☐☐☐☐☐☐☐☐☐☐☐☐☐☐☐
☐☐☐☐☐☐☐☐☐☐☐☐☐☐☐☐

28 ☐☐☐☐☐☐☐☐☐☐☐☐☐☐☐☐☐
☐☐☐☐☐☐☐☐☐☐☐☐☐☐☐☐

29 ☐☐☐☐☐☐☐☐☐☐☐☐☐☐☐☐☐
☐☐☐☐☐☐☐☐☐☐☐☐☐☐☐☐

30 ☐☐☐☐☐☐☐☐☐☐☐☐☐☐☐☐☐
☐☐☐☐☐☐☐☐☐☐☐☐☐☐☐☐

Cambridge
C1 Advanced
Use of English

Test 2

Part 1

For questions 1–8, read the text below and decide which answer best fits each gap. In the separate answer sheet, mark the appropriate answer (A, B, C or D).

The Eiffel Tower

The Eiffel Tower was designed by the French engineer, Gustave Eiffel, and was built between 1887 and 1889 to commemorate the centenary of the French Revolution. Eiffel's vision and engineering prowess has resulted in a **(1)**_____ that has become one of the most visited tourist attractions in the world. It is estimated that over 250 million people have visited the tower since it was built, and it has been featured in countless movies and **(2)**_____ of art and has inspired many artists and designers.

Gustave Eiffel was a renowned engineer and designer of his time. He was **(3)**_____ for the construction of many bridges and railway stations in France. The Eiffel Tower was his most **(4)**_____ project and was designed to be the tallest structure in the world at the time. At 324 metres tall and weighing approximately 10,000 tons, it has three observation decks that offer spectacular views of Paris. The tower is also **(5)**_____ to several restaurants, including the Michelin-starred restaurant, Jules Verne.

The construction process was a remarkable feat **(6)**_____ engineering. Over 300 workers were involved in it. A system of cranes and pulleys that workers to transport materials and equipment to the top of the tower was used. The construction process was also **(7)**_____ for its safety record. Despite the height of the tower, there were no fatalities during the construction process.

The tower's importance to French culture and history cannot be overstated, and it will undoubtedly inspire and **(8)**_____ people for generations to come.

1	**A** building	**B** structure	**C** house	**D** property
2	**A** works	**B** designs	**C** products	**D** creations
3	**A** control	**B** responsible	**C** charge	**D** director
4	**A** cautious	**B** driven	**C** progressive	**D** ambitious
5	**A** place	**B** local	**C** home	**D** situated
6	**A** on	**B** about	**C** with	**D** of
7	**A** notable	**B** indicated	**C** pronounced	**D** recognisable
8	**A** appreciate	**B** admire	**C** captivate	**D** praise

Part 2

For questions 9–16, read the text below and decide which word best fits each gap. Use only one word for each gap. In the separate answer sheet, write your answers in capital letters, using one box per letter.

Live in the moment

'Live in the moment' is a phrase often used to encourage people to focus their attention on the present moment and to enjoy the experiences that they are having 'right now'. It's a reminder to appreciate the here and now, rather than getting caught **(9)**_____ in worries about the future or regrets about the past.

Living in the moment can **(10)**_____ many benefits for our mental and emotional well-being. **(11)**_____ focusing our attention on the present moment, we can reduce stress and anxiety, improve our ability to concentrate and increase our overall sense of happiness and contentment.

However, it's important to note that living in the moment doesn't **(12)**_____ ignoring the past or neglecting the future. It simply means being present and fully engaged in the current moment, while also learning from the **(13)**_____ and planning for the future.

So, take a deep **(14)**_____, look around you and try to appreciate the beauty and wonder of the present moment. Whether you're spending time with loved **(15)**_____, enjoying a beautiful sunset or simply savouring a delicious meal, make the most of the experience and cherish **(16)**_____ moment we are given.

Part 3

For questions 17–24, use the stem word on the right to form the correct word that fills each gap. In the separate answer sheet, write your answers in capital letters, using one box per letter.

The differences between dolphins, whales and porpoises

While dolphins, whales and porpoises share many similarities with aquatic mammals, there are notable differences in their physical **(17)**_____, behaviour and diet that set them apart from each other. They are all aquatic mammals that belong to the same group called cetaceans.

CHARACTER

One of the biggest differences between the three is their physical appearance. Dolphins are generally smaller than whales, with a **(18)**_____ of about 3 to 9 feet, while whales can grow up to 100 feet. Porpoises, on the other hand, are much smaller than both dolphins and whales, ranging from 4 to 6 feet.

LONG

Another **(19)**_____ is the shape of their snouts. Dolphins have elongated, pointed snouts, whereas porpoises have shorter, more rounded snouts. Whales, meanwhile, have a much broader head with a blunt snout.

DISTINCT

(20)_____, dolphins and porpoises are more social than whales. They live in groups called 'pods', and often exhibit playful behaviour, such as leaping out of the water or riding the waves of boats. Whales, however, are more solitary and less playful, and typically travel alone or in small groups.

BEHAVIOUR

Another significant difference is their diet. Dolphins and porpoises **(21)**_____ feed on fish and squid, while whales are known to consume large amounts of krill and other small marine creatures.

PRIME

In terms of **(22)**_____ status, all three species face various threats, including habitat loss, hunting, pollution and climate change. However, some species of whales, such as the blue whale, are considered **(23)**_____ while others, such as dolphins and porpoises, are relatively more abundant.

CONSERVE

DANGER

Understanding such differences can help us to **(24)**_____ appreciate and protect these magnificent creatures.

GOOD

Part 4

For questions 25–30, complete the second sentence, using the word given, so that it has a similar meaning to the first sentence. **Do not change the word provided and use between three and six words in total.** In the separate answer sheet, write your answers in capital letters, using one box per letter.

25 I have never had such a bad cup of coffee.

BEFORE

Never _____ such a bad cup of coffee.

26 The new speeding fines haven't stopped people from speeding.

INEFFECTIVE

The new speeding fines are _____ people from speeding.

27 If it is cancelled, the football game will take place at a later date.

BEING

In the event _____, the football game will place at a later date.

28 His teacher said that he was failing the course.

DANGER

His teacher said that he was _____ failing the course.

29 Ahmed wanted to ask if he could be transferred to another office.

REQUEST

Ahmed wanted to put _____ a transfer to another office.

30 The manager spoke for ages about nothing during the meeting.

POINT

It took ages for the manager to _____ during the meeting.

Answer sheet: Cambridge C1 Advanced
Use of English

Test No.

Mark out of 36

Name _____   **Date** _____

Part 1: Multiple choice

8 marks

Mark the appropriate answer (A, B, C or D).

0	A	B	C	D

1	A	B	C	D		5	A	B	C	D
2	A	B	C	D		6	A	B	C	D
3	A	B	C	D		7	A	B	C	D
4	A	B	C	D		8	A	B	C	D

Part 2: Open cloze

8 marks

Write your answers in capital letters, using one box per letter.

0	B	E	C	A	U	S	E				

9											
10											
11											
12											
13											
14											
15											
16											

Part 3: Word formation

Write your answers in capital letters, using one box per letter.

17

18

19

20

21

22

23

24

Part 4: Key word transformation

Write your answers in capital letters, using one box per letter.

25

26

27

28

29

30

Cambridge
C1 Advanced
Use of English

Test 3

Part 1

For questions 1–8, read the text below and decide which answer best fits each gap. In the separate answer sheet, mark the appropriate answer (A, B, C or D).

Translation Technology

In recent years, translation technology has **(1)**_____ rapidly, leading to the development of applications and **(2)**_____ tools that have transformed the way translations are conducted. So, what impact has this technological **(3)**_____ had on human translators, and what are the benefits for the wider community?

The earliest form of translation technology was a simple machine translation tools, which could only translate basic sentences. Over time, more advanced translation tools were developed, such as computer-assisted translation (CAT) software, which can **(4)**_____ translations in a database and suggest translations for new text based on previous ones.

Another significant development has been the **(5)**_____ of neural machine translation (NMT). NMT uses artificial intelligence (AI) and deep learning to translate text more accurately than previous methods.

However, the impact of translation technology on human translators has been mixed. On the one hand, it has made their work more efficient and **(6)**_____, allowing them to focus on the creative aspects of translation rather than repetitive tasks. On the other hand, some translators are **(7)**_____ about technology potentially replacing them altogether, particularly as AI continues to advance.

Despite these concerns, translation technology has many benefits for the wider community. It has made translation services more affordable and accessible, as well as helping break down language **(8)**_____ and promoting global communication and understanding.

1	**A**	evolved	**B**	converted	**C**	benefited	**D**	released
2	**A**	innovative	**B**	gifted	**C**	customary	**D**	conventional
3	**A**	disaster	**B**	revolution	**C**	rebellion	**D**	establishment
4	**A**	store	**B**	supply	**C**	collect	**D**	prolong
5	**A**	reign	**B**	rise	**C**	raise	**D**	rendering
6	**A**	enlarged	**B**	analysed	**C**	streamlined	**D**	trimmed
7	**A**	eager	**B**	agitated	**C**	diligent	**D**	apprehensive
8	**A**	boundaries	**B**	barriers	**C**	borders	**D**	perimeters

Part 2

For questions 9–16, read the text below and decide which word best fits each gap. Use only one word for each gap. In the separate answer sheet, write your answers in capital letters, using one box per letter.

La Almudena Cathedral

La Almudena Cathedral is a unique masterpiece located in the heart of Madrid, Spain. It is considered one of the most significant religious buildings in the country, and its construction lasted **(9)**_____ a century, beginning in 1879 and ending in 1993.

The Cathedral's facade has **(10)**_____ different styles: the neoclassical front and the neo-gothic rear. The latter features an incredible dome that rises up to the sky, measuring over 100 meters in **(11)**_____, making it one of the most notable features of the building. The interior of the Cathedral is also awe-inspiring, with a vast central nave that stands **(12)**_____ for its size and beauty.

One of the Cathedral's most interesting aspects is its history. It was built on the site **(13)**_____ a mosque, which was later converted into a church, and finally into the structure that stands today. The construction of the Cathedral was long and complicated, with numerous setbacks and delays, including the Spanish Civil War, which halted work **(14)**_____ many years.

Despite its relatively recent completion, La Almudena Cathedral has already become an iconic symbol of Madrid, and an important pilgrimage destination for Catholics. Its **(15)**_____ proximity to the Royal Palace makes it a popular tourist destination as well. Overall, La Almudena Cathedral is a must-see for anyone interested in history, architecture or religion, and it is sure to leave a lasting impression on **(16)**_____ who visit.

Part 3

For questions 17–24, use the stem word on the right to form the correct word that fills each gap. In the separate answer sheet, write your answers in capital letters, using one box per letter.

Male hair loss

Male baldness is a prevalent condition that affects men across all age groups. It is characterised by progressive hair loss that begins with a receding hairline and **(17)**_____ hair on the crown of the head. While the natural ageing process is a primary cause, male baldness can also be attributed to several factors.

THIN

One of the causes of male baldness is **(18)**_____ inheritance. Studies have shown that male-pattern baldness is closely related to **(19)**_____ genes that men inherit from their parents. Other contributors to male baldness include stress, nutritional deficiencies and medical conditions or medications. For instance, thyroid issues, autoimmune **(20)**_____ and chemotherapy can lead to hair loss in men.

GENE

SPECIFY

ORDER

In recent years, baldness has gained **(21)**_____ as a fashion statement, with many men embracing it as a symbol of masculinity and self-confidence. This trend has been **(22)**_____ by notable figures such as actors Dwayne 'The Rock' Johnson and Vin Diesel.

ACCEPT

POPULAR

Nevertheless, it is crucial to note that not all men are comfortable with baldness, and some may experience a negative impact on their self-esteem and mental **(23)**_____ as a result. Seeking appropriate treatments and support can help improve their self-esteem and overall quality of life. Additionally, various treatments such as a hair transplant, scalp micropigmentation and medication can be **(24)**_____.

WELL

ADVANCE

Part 4

For questions 25–30, complete the second sentence, using the word given, so that it has a similar meaning to the first sentence. Do not change the word provided and use between three and six words in total. In the separate answer sheet, write your answers in capital letters, using one box per letter.

25 Can you believe that she spent more than £50 on her new dress?

LESS

Can you believe that she spent _____ £50 on her new dress?

26 We don't expect him to pass the exam.

HOPE

We don't hold _____ that he will pass the exam.

27 The situation they were in was a potential danger for the police officers.

PUT

The police officers were _____ by the situation they were in.

28 What made you think that Jamie would get the job?

LED

What was it that _____ that Jamie would get the job?

29 It looks like she has forgotten about our meeting.

TO

She seems _____ about our meeting.

30 Playing football is fun, but so is playing rugby.

JUST

It's _____ fun playing football, as it is rugby.

Answer sheet: Cambridge C1 Advanced
Use of English

Test No. [ ]

Mark out of 36 [ ]

Name _____   Date _____

Part 1: Multiple choice

8 marks

Mark the appropriate answer (A, B, C or D).

0	A	B	C	D

1	A	B	C	D		5	A	B	C	D
2	A	B	C	D		6	A	B	C	D
3	A	B	C	D		7	A	B	C	D
4	A	B	C	D		8	A	B	C	D

Part 2: Open cloze

8 marks

Write your answers in capital letters, using one box per letter.

0	B	E	C	A	U	S	E				

9											
10											
11											
12											
13											
14											
15											
16											

Part 3: Word formation

8 marks

Write your answers in capital letters, using one box per letter.

17											
18											
19											
20											
21											
22											
23											
24											

Part 4: Key word transformation

12 marks

Write your answers in capital letters, using one box per letter.

25																		
26																		
27																		
28																		
29																		
30																		

Cambridge C1 Advanced Use of English

Test 4

Part 1

For questions 1–8, read the text below and decide which answer best fits each gap. In the separate answer sheet, mark the appropriate answer (A, B, C or D).

The secret of Irish charm

The Blarney Stone located in the village of Blarney, County Cork, Ireland, and is a highly **(1)**_____ tourist attraction. This historic stone's mystical properties have attracted visitors from all over the world for centuries.

According to **(2)**_____, kissing the Blarney Stone will provide the kisser with the gift of eloquence, or fluent and persuasive speech. The stone is a block of bluestone, and visitors must lean backwards to kiss it. The **(3)**_____ can be nerve-wracking – it requires leaning back over a gap in the wall many metres above the ground – but the reward of gaining the rights to say you've done it is **(4)**_____ worth the risk.

The Blarney Stone has been an iconic symbol of Ireland for centuries. **(5)**_____ the years, many famous people have kissed the Blarney Stone, including Winston Churchill, who famously stated that visiting was 'worth the journey to Ireland alone'.

Aside from the Blarney Stone, Blarney Castle itself is a stunning **(6)**_____ to behold. The castle dates back to the 15th century and was built by the MacCarthy dynasty. The castle is **(7)**_____ by magnificent gardens, which have been carefully tended to for hundreds of years.

The Blarney Stone is a unique and fascinating tourist attraction **(8)**_____ in rich history, that visitors from all over the world continue to check it out on their visit to Ireland.

1	**A**	received	**B**	sought	**C**	revered	**D**	distinguished
2	**A**	folk	**B**	narration	**C**	fable	**D**	legend
3	**A**	process	**B**	action	**C**	case	**D**	mechanism
4	**A**	assured	**B**	better	**C**	much	**D**	well
5	**A**	With	**B**	All	**C**	Throughout	**D**	Across
6	**A**	sight	**B**	look	**C**	visual	**D**	picture
7	**A**	alongside	**B**	surrounded	**C**	circled	**D**	placed
8	**A**	soaked	**B**	steeped	**C**	located	**D**	understood

Part 2

For questions 9–16, read the text below and decide which word best fits each gap. Use only one word for each gap. In the separate answer sheet, write your answers in capital letters, using one box per letter.

Saving for a rainy day

Saving money is an important aspect of personal finance that everyone should practise. A 'rainy-day fund' is a name given to money that is set aside for unforeseen expenses such as unexpected car or home repairs and medical bills or job loss. In an ideal world, it is something that every household should **(9)**_____, and it can provide financial security during tough times.

Sudden expenses can, by definition, come out **(10)**_____ nowhere and cause a financial strain on a family. For example, if your car **(11)**_____ down you need to have it repaired to get to work or run errands. Home repairs such as a leaky roof, plumbing issues or electrical problems can **(12)**_____ a lot of money, and job loss can be financially devastating. It may require you to dip into your 'rainy day fund' until you find new employment.

It is rather worrying to note that a survey of Americans found that 50% of the adult population had very little or no savings at **(13)**_____, and their only solution to an unexpected cost would be getting into debt. This has been attributed to very high costs of **(14)**_____ and little financial literacy.

So, it's important to have some money set **(15)**_____ for a rainy day, and to make saving a priority. Experts recommend having three-to-six months of expenses saved in **(16)**_____ a fund. This can help you weather unexpected financial storms and provide a sense of financial security.

Part 3

For questions 17–24, use the stem word on the right to form the correct word that fills each gap. In the separate answer sheet, write your answers in capital letters, using one box per letter.

TikTok

TikTok is a social media platform that allows users to create short videos of themselves that can be edited using music, filters and effects. The rise of TikTok can be attributed to its appeal to younger audiences who enjoy its user-friendly **(17)**_____, entertaining content and opportunities for self-expression.   **FACE**

TikTok has quickly become a **(18)**_____   **CULTURE**
phenomenon, with its popularity skyrocketing in recent years. As of 2021, the app has over one billion active users worldwide, making it one of the most popular social media platforms in the world. Its popularity has also **(19)**_____ to the rise of   **LEAD**
'TikTok influencers' who use the platform to reach large audiences and promote products and services.

The app has become particularly popular among teenagers and young adults who appreciate its **(20)**_____ to   **ABLE**
showcase their creativity, humour and talents. TikTok's algorithm also plays a significant role in the **(21)**_____   **WIDE**
of success, as it allows users to discover new content that is tailored to their interests and preferences.

TikTok's rise has not been without **(22)**_____,   **CONTROVERSIAL**
however. Some have raised concerns about the app's potential to compromise user privacy and its potential to spread **(23)**_____. Despite these concerns, TikTok continues   **INFORM**
to be in **(24)**_____ use among all ages, all over the   **SPREAD**
world.

Part 4

For questions 25–30, complete the second sentence, using the word given, so that it has a similar meaning to the first sentence. Do not change the word provided and use between three and six words in total. In the separate answer sheet, write your answers in capital letters, using one box per letter.

25 Joaquin wanted to know how to make his dream a reality.

TRUE

Joaquin wanted to know how to make his _____.

26 It's my parent's 50th wedding anniversary next week.

MARRIED

Next week my parents _____ for 50 years.

27 Even though the company offered him a job, Jacob still didn't want it.

DESPITE

Jacob still didn't want the job, _____ him it.

28 In the task, you must speak for two minutes without stopping.

REQUIRED

In the task, you _____ two minutes without stopping.

29 I'm very sorry, I didn't realise how late it was.

TRACK

Sorry, I completely _____ the time.

30 Alison hoped the play would be more interesting than it actually was.

NOT

The play was _____ Alison had hoped.

Mark out of 36

Name _____ **Date** _____

Part 1: Multiple choice

8 marks

Mark the appropriate answer (A, B, C or D).

0	A	B	C	D
	—	■	—	—

1	A	B	C	D		5	A	B	C	D
	—	—	—	—			—	—	—	—

2	A	B	C	D		6	A	B	C	D
	—	—	—	—			—	—	—	—

3	A	B	C	D		7	A	B	C	D
	—	—	—	—			—	—	—	—

4	A	B	C	D		8	A	B	C	D
	—	—	—	—			—	—	—	—

Part 2: Open cloze

8 marks

Write your answers in capital letters, using one box per letter.

0	B	E	C	A	U	S	E				

9											
10											
11											
12											
13											
14											
15											
16											

Part 3: Word formation

Write your answers in capital letters, using one box per letter.

17										
18										
19										
20										
21										
22										
23										
24										

Part 4: Key word transformation

Write your answers in capital letters, using one box per letter.

25																		

26																		

27																		

28																		

29																		

30																		

Cambridge
C1 Advanced
Use of English

Test 5

Part 1

For questions 1–8, read the text below and decide which answer best fits each gap. In the separate answer sheet, mark the appropriate answer (A, B, C or D).

Parkinson's Disease

Parkinson's Disease is a disorder that affects the central nervous system, specifically certain cells in the brain. The condition primarily affects movement, causing symptoms such as stiffness, slowness of movement and difficulties with balance and coordination. It is chronic and **(1)**_____, meaning that symptoms worsen over time.

The development of Parkinson's Disease is **(2)**_____ to be caused by a combination of genetic and environmental factors. The exact cause of the condition is unknown, but it is believed to involve a loss of dopamine production in the brain. Dopamine is a neurotransmitter that plays a key **(3)**_____ in the regulation of movement and emotion.

The treatment of Parkinson's Disease has **(4)**_____ significant development over the years. The first effective treatment for the condition was the drug L-dopa, which can help to **(5)**_____ the brain's dopamine supply. While L-dopa can provide significant symptom relief, it is not a **(6)**_____ for Parkinson's and can have side effects such as abnormal involuntary movements.

Other drugs have since been developed to treat Parkinson's disease, which **(7)**_____ the effects of dopamine in the brain, as well as research into stem cell therapy. **(8)**_____ stem cell therapy is still in the early stages of development, it holds promise as a potential future treatment option for Parkinson's disease.

1	**A**	measured	**B**	passive	**C**	moderate	**D**	progressive
2	**A**	informed	**B**	thought	**C**	convinced	**D**	threatened
3	**A**	role	**B**	character	**C**	position	**D**	responsibility
4	**A**	enacted	**B**	conducted	**C**	tackled	**D**	undergone
5	**A**	magnify	**B**	fill	**C**	administer	**D**	replenish
6	**A**	symptom	**B**	cure	**C**	prescription	**D**	condition
7	**A**	mimic	**B**	portray	**C**	convey	**D**	signal
8	**A**	Despite	**B**	While	**C**	But	**D**	However

Part 2

For questions 9–16, read the text below and decide which word best fits each gap. Use only one word for each gap. In the separate answer sheet, write your answers in capital letters, using one box per letter.

A Digital Time Out

In today's digital age, it seems impossible to stay disconnected from the world for even a few hours. People are glued to their mobile phones, checking emails, scrolling **(9)**_____ social media and responding to text messages. However, it is crucial to switch off mobile phones for a day **(10**_____ in a while to disconnect from the digital world and reconnect with the real world.

Firstly, switching off mobile phones for a day can reduce stress and anxiety levels. The constant notifications and alerts from mobile phones can cause distractions, resulting in reduced productivity levels and increased stress. By disconnecting from the digital world, people can enjoy a day of **(11)**_____ and quiet, which can help to improve mental health.

Secondly, switching your phone off for a while can improve interpersonal relationships. By putting aside their devices, people can focus on spending quality time with family and friends, having meaningful conversations and engaging **(12)**_____ activities that they enjoy together. This can lead **(13)**_____ improved overall well-being.

Lastly, powering down your smartphone for a day every **(14)**_____ and then, even for a few hours **(15)**_____ so, can improve sleep quality. The blue light emitted by mobile phones can disrupt the circadian rhythm, making it difficult to **(16)**_____ asleep and stay asleep. By disconnecting from the digital world, people can reduce exposure to 'blue light' and enjoy a good night's sleep, and wake up feeling refreshed and ready for the day ahead.

Part 3

For questions 17–24, use the stem word on the right to form the correct word that fills each gap. In the separate answer sheet, write your answers in capital letters, using one box per letter.

Switching off the internet

If we were to switch off the internet, life would undoubtedly change **(17)**_____. We would be transported back to an era of analogue living, where communication and information exchange was limited to physical interactions and written **(18)**_____.

DRAMA

CORRESPOND

Without the internet, we would have to rely on traditional means of communication such as postal mail, telephone and face-to-face conversations. This shift would require us to slow down and be more intentional in our interactions, allowing us to develop **(19)**_____ and more meaningful relationships. It could also encourage us to be more present in the moment and appreciate the here and now.

DEEP

However, there would also be significant **(20)**_____. Without the internet, for instance, we would **(21)**_____ access to a wealth of information and resources that is currently at our fingertips. Online shopping, banking and entertainment would no longer be possible, **(22)**_____ us to adapt to a more analogue lifestyle. We may have to go back to visiting physical stores, banks and entertainment venues, which could be both **(23)**_____ and time-consuming.

DRAW

LOSS

FORCE

CONVENIENCE

Switching off the internet would have both positive and negative consequences. While it may encourage a more 'back to basics' approach to life and intense interpersonal connections, it would also provide **(24)**_____ to our access to information and modern conveniences.

LIMIT

Part 4

For questions 25–30, complete the second sentence, using the word given, so that it has a similar meaning to the first sentence. Do not change the word provided and use between three and six words in total. In the separate answer sheet, write your answers in capital letters, using one box per letter.

25 Hwan fully intends to do his homework.

EVERY

Hwan has _____ doing his homework.

26 They spent a long time solving the problem.

FIGURE

It took them a long time _____ the problem.

27 Asif will fix the bathroom sink when he has time.

ROUND

Asif will _____ the bathroom sink when he has time.

28 Someone was driving the car very quickly, the police said.

BEING

The police said that the car _____ very quickly.

29 "Are you staying for dinner?" Heath asked Sophie.

STAYING

Heath asked Sophie _____ for dinner.

30 If you really want to move abroad, there is nothing I can say to stop you.

INSIST

If you _____ abroad, there is nothing I can say to stop you.

Mark out of 36

Name _____ **Date** _____

Part 1: Multiple choice

8 marks

Mark the appropriate answer (A, B, C or D).

0	A	B	C	D

1	A	B	C	D
2	A	B	C	D
3	A	B	C	D
4	A	B	C	D

5	A	B	C	D
6	A	B	C	D
7	A	B	C	D
8	A	B	C	D

Part 2: Open cloze

8 marks

Write your answers in capital letters, using one box per letter.

0	B	E	C	A	U	S	E				

9											
10											
11											
12											
13											
14											
15											
16											

Part 3: Word formation

Write your answers in capital letters, using one box per letter.

17											
18											
19											
20											
21											
22											
23											
24											

Part 4: Key word transformation

Write your answers in capital letters, using one box per letter.

25																		
26																		
27																		
28																		
29																		
30																		

Cambridge
C1 Advanced
Use of English

Test 6

Part 1

For questions 1–8, read the text below and decide which answer best fits each gap. In the separate answer sheet, mark the appropriate answer (A, B, C or D).

Internet security advice

As the internet is an integral part of our lives, it's important to take steps to protect ourselves from the many security threats that exist online. Here are some general internet security **(1)**_____ that can help keep you safe:

1. Keep your software updated: Updates often include security 'patches' that fix known **(2)**_____ such as areas where your computer may be open to hacking or being attacked. It's important to keep your software, especially your operating system and antivirus software, up to date.
2. Be cautious of emails and links: Phishing emails and links can trick you into **(3)**_____ away sensitive information or downloading malware. Be **(4)**_____ to emails or links from unfamiliar sources, and never send personal information unless you're sure it's in response to a legitimate request.
3. Use two-factor authentication: Two-factor authentication adds an extra **(5)**_____ of security to your accounts by requiring a code, usually sent to your phone, in addition to your password.
4. Use a Virtual Private Network (VPN): A VPN can help **(6)**_____ your online privacy and security by encrypting your internet traffic and hiding your IP address.
5. Be cautious of public wi-fi: Public wi-fi networks can be easy targets for hackers, so avoid using **(7)**_____ for sensitive activities like banking or shopping.

By following these tips, you can keep your personal information and online identity safe and secure and reduce your risk of falling **(8)**_____ to internet security threats.

1	**A** requirements	**B** orders	**C** tips	**D** advice
2	**A** defenses	**B** vulnerabilities	**C** exposure	**D** sensitivities
3	**A** handing	**B** offering	**C** giving	**D** sending
4	**A** alert	**B** anxious	**C** alarmed	**D** attentive
5	**A** layer	**B** volume	**C** proportion	**D** extent
6	**A** save	**B** protect	**C** guard	**D** stop
7	**A** it	**B** them	**C** that	**D** him
8	**A** object	**B** target	**C** aim	**D** victim

Part 2

For questions 9–16, read the text below and decide which word best fits each gap. Use only one word for each gap. In the separate answer sheet, write your answers in capital letters, using one box per letter.

TV remote controls

TV remote controls **(9)**_____ invented in the 1950s to solve a common problem that TV viewers faced – the need to manually adjust the television's settings.

Before remote controls, viewers had to get up and physically turn knobs to change the channel or adjust the volume. This was **(10)**_____ only inconvenient but also disruptive **(11)**_____ the viewing experience.

The first TV remote controls used ultrasonic signals to communicate with the television set. They were expensive and not very reliable, but they paved the way for the development of infrared (IR) remote controls, which are **(12)**_____ widely used today. IR remote controls use light to send signals to the TV, allowing viewers to control their TV sets from **(13)**_____ distance. This technology revolutionised the **(14)**_____ in which we interact with our TVs and made watching TV a more comfortable and enjoyable experience.

Remote controls have since evolved to include advanced features such as voice control and **(15)**_____-screen technology. They have also become more affordable and accessible, allowing more people to enjoy the convenience of controlling their TVs from far away. They are now indispensable tools in our daily lives, making watching TV a **(16)**_____ comfortable and enjoyable experience.

Part 3

For questions 17–24, use the stem word on the right to form the correct word that fills each gap. In the separate answer sheet, write your answers in capital letters, using one box per letter.

Ms. Marvel

I was thrilled to discover the latest addition to the Marvel universe – 'Ms. Marvel'. This show, which streamed on Disney Plus, is an important **(17)**_____ to the Marvel Universe, as it breaks away from the traditional superhero mould.

ADD

Kamala Khan, the teenage girl who takes on the role of Ms. Marvel, is not your 'typical' hero. She is a Muslim, Pakistani-American girl who struggles with the challenges of being a teenager in today's society. This **(18)**_____ and representation is significant, as it allows audiences to see themselves **(19)**_____ on screen.

DIVERSE

REFLECT

Another reason why 'Ms. Marvel' is so important is the way it challenges the usual **(20)**_____ of superhero stories. The show's focus on everyday issues, such as **(21)**_____ in and finding one's place in the world, is a **(22)**_____ change from the usual focus on epic battles and world-ending threats. This shift in focus allows audiences to connect with the characters on a more personal level, creating a **(23)**_____ emotional resonance with the story.

NARRATE

FIT

FRESH

DEEP

In short, Ms. Marvel is not just a superhero show – it is a celebration representation, shows the realities of the world, and the power of **(24)**_____ storytelling.

RELATE

Part 4

For questions 25–30, complete the second sentence, using the word given, so that it has a similar meaning to the first sentence. Do not change the word provided and use between three and six words in total. In the separate answer sheet, write your answers in capital letters, using one box per letter.

25   We paid a photographer to take a photograph of us at the water park.

HAD

At the water park we _____ by a photographer.

26   It's possible that Miguel came round while you were out.

MAY

Miguel _____ while you were out.

27   Don't tell anyone about what I said about Tom.

KEEP

Please _____ yourself about what I said to Tom.

28   She tried hard to finish her work by the end of the day.

BEST

She _____ to finish her work by the end of the day.

29   Could you speak French two years ago?

ABLE

Two years ago, _____ to speak French?

30   Feng had plans this evening, but her friend cancelled.

THROUGH

Feng's plans _____ this evening because her friend cancelled.

Answer sheet: Cambridge C1 Advanced
Use of English

Test No.

Mark out of 36

Name _____   **Date** _____

Part 1: Multiple choice

8 marks

Mark the appropriate answer (A, B, C or D).

| 0 | A | B | C | D | |

1	A	B	C	D
2	A	B	C	D
3	A	B	C	D
4	A	B	C	D

5	A	B	C	D
6	A	B	C	D
7	A	B	C	D
8	A	B	C	D

Part 2: Open cloze

8 marks

Write your answers in capital letters, using one box per letter.

| 0 | B | E | C | A | U | S | E | | | | |

9											
10											
11											
12											
13											
14											
15											
16											

Part 3: Word formation

Write your answers in capital letters, using one box per letter.

17										
18										
19										
20										
21										
22										
23										
24										

Part 4: Key word transformation

12 marks

Write your answers in capital letters, using one box per letter.

25																	
26																	
27																	
28																	
29																	
30																	

Cambridge
C1 Advanced
Use of English

Test 7

Part 1

For questions 1–8, read the text below and decide which answer best fits each gap. In the separate answer sheet, mark the appropriate answer (A, B, C or D).

The Star Wars franchise on Disney Plus

The Star Wars franchise has been one of the most popular and enduring sci-fi franchises in history. With a massive fan base that spans multiple generations, it's no surprise that Disney Plus has been capitalising on the **(1)**_____ of the franchise with its Star Wars content.

One of the biggest draws for fans of the franchise is undoubtedly the highly acclaimed live-action series 'The Mandalorian'. The show, **(2)**_____ follows the adventures of a lone bounty hunter and his charge, Baby Yoda, has been **(3)**_____ for its stunning visuals, gripping storytelling and **(4)**_____ characters.

In addition to 'The Mandalorian', Disney Plus also offers several other Star Wars shows, including the animated series 'The Clone Wars and Rebels', as well as the new animated series 'The Bad Batch'. These shows provide fans with **(5)**_____ more opportunities to explore the rich and varied universe of Star Wars.

But it's not just about the shows on Disney Plus – the streaming service also offers access to all of the Star Wars movies. This **(6)**_____ that fans can enjoy the entire saga in one place, and with the added bonus of additional behind-the-scenes content.

Overall, Disney Plus has done an excellent **(7)**_____ of catering to the vast and diverse fanbase of the Star Wars franchise. With its selection of shows, movies and additional content, fans have plenty of reasons to **(8)**_____ glued to their screens for hours on end.

1	**A**	fame	**B**	popularity	**C**	demand	**D**	welcome
2	**A**	what	**B**	which	**C**	when	**D**	who
3	**A**	praised	**B**	celebrated	**C**	worshipped	**D**	loved
4	**A**	comparative	**B**	compiling	**C**	continual	**D**	compelling
5	**A**	always	**B**	similar	**C**	even	**D**	so
6	**A**	intends	**B**	means	**C**	plans	**D**	aims
7	**A**	role	**B**	post	**C**	job	**D**	work
8	**A**	stay	**B**	keep	**C**	leave	**D**	hold

Part 2

For questions 9–16, read the text below and decide which word best fits each gap. Use only one word for each gap. In the separate answer sheet, write your answers in capital letters, using one box per letter.

The Stone of Destiny

The Stone of Scone, also known as the Stone of Destiny, is a block of sandstone that has been a symbol of Scottish royalty for centuries. **(9)**_____ is said to have been used as a coronation stone for Scottish kings during the early Middle Ages.

The Stone of Scone was originally **(10)**_____ at the monastery of Scone in Scotland. It was used in the coronation ceremonies of Scottish kings, including Kenneth MacAlpin, who was crowned **(11)**_____ the stone in the 9th century. The stone was believed to have been brought to Scotland from Ireland, where it was used **(12)**_____ a sacred stone in the coronation of Irish kings.

In 1296, the English king Edward I invaded Scotland and took the Stone of Scone **(13)**_____ to England. It was then placed in Westminster Abbey in London, where it was used in the coronation ceremonies of English monarchs. The Stone of Scone remained in Westminster Abbey for over 700 years, **(14)**_____ 1950, when a group of Scottish nationalists stole it and returned it to Scotland.

The importance of the Stone of Scone lies in **(15)**_____ symbolism of Scottish independence and sovereignty. The stone's history and cultural significance have made it an important **(16)**_____ of Scottish identity and a symbol of national pride. The stone continues to be an important symbol of Scottish culture and heritage to this day.

Part 3

For questions 17–24, use the stem word on the right to form the correct word that fills each gap. In the separate answer sheet, write your answers in capital letters, using one box per letter.

Growing a Revolution

Growing a Revolution by David R. Montgomery is an insightful book that offers a fresh perspective on sustainable agriculture. Montgomery, a **(17)**_____ geologist, presents a compelling argument for regenerative farming practices, emphasising the benefits of soil health and biodiversity.

KNOWN

The book begins by highlighting the problems associated with modern agriculture, including soil **(18)**_____, water pollution and greenhouse gas emissions. Montgomery then takes the reader on a journey around the world, visiting farmers who have implemented regenerative practices and achieved **(19)**_____ results.

GRADE

REMARK

Montgomery's writing style is clear and engaging, and he uses real-life examples to illustrate his points **(20)**_____. This helps readers understand the main ideas quickly and encourages them to read to the end of the book. He also provides practical advice on how farmers can transition to regenerative practices, stressing the importance of experimentation and **(21)**_____.

EFFECTIVE

ADAPT

One of the book's key **(22)**_____ is its emphasis on the importance of soil health. Montgomery claims that healthy soil is the foundation of this type of agriculture, and he provides a detailed **(23)**_____ of the science behind this claim. He also discusses the importance of **(24)**_____ stating how it can help to improve soil health and reduce the need for synthetic inputs. This book is a key read for anyone from gardeners to farmers growing crops for your supermarkets.

STRONG

ANALYSE

DIVERSE

Part 4

For questions 25–30, complete the second sentence, using the word given, so that it has a similar meaning to the first sentence. Do not change the word provided and use between three and six words in total. In the separate answer sheet, write your answers in capital letters, using one box per letter.

25 They got married a year ago today.

TIME

They got married _____ year.

26 Ray is usually very chatty, it's strange to see him so quiet.

LIKE

It's strange that Ray was so quiet; it's _____, he is usually very chatty.

27 As it got darker, it became more difficult for me to see.

HARDER

The darker _____ it became for me to see.

28 "I won't tolerate his behaviour anymore," Jennie said.

UP

Jennie said that she would not _____ anymore.

29 Would you mind watering my plants while I'm on holiday?

WONDERING

I _____ you would water my plants while I was on holiday?

30 It doesn't matter what you say because I won't change my mind.

DIFFERENCE

It doesn't _____ what you said because I won't change my mind.

Test No.

Mark out of 36

Name _____   Date _____

Part 1: Multiple choice

8 marks

Mark the appropriate answer (A, B, C or D).

0	A	B	C	D
	—	▬	—	—

1	A	B	C	D		5	A	B	C	D
2	A	B	C	D		6	A	B	C	D
3	A	B	C	D		7	A	B	C	D
4	A	B	C	D		8	A	B	C	D

Part 2: Open cloze

8 marks

Write your answers in capital letters, using one box per letter.

| 0 | B | E | C | A | U | S | E | | | | |

9											
10											
11											
12											
13											
14											
15											
16											

Part 3: Word formation

Write your answers in capital letters, using one box per letter.

17

18

19

20

21

22

23

24

Part 4: Key word transformation

Write your answers in capital letters, using one box per letter.

25

26

27

28

29

30

Cambridge
C1 Advanced
Use of English

Test 8

Part 1

For questions 1–8, read the text below and decide which answer best fits each gap. In the separate answer sheet, mark the appropriate answer (A, B, C or D).

Why libraries are so important

Libraries play a crucial role in our society for a variety of reasons. They **(1)**_____ access to a wide range of information resources, including books, journals, newspapers, magazines and online databases. This access to information is essential for people **(2)**_____ all ages to learn and grow. Libraries are essential to education at all levels **(3)**_____ resources for students, from pre-schoolers to graduate students, as well as programmes and events that promote reading and writing, also known as **(4)**_____.

Libraries are often a hub of community activity. They offer a place for people to gather, learn and share ideas. Many libraries also host community events, such as book clubs, author readings and writing workshops. What's more, most of these sessions are free of charge, or have a very low entry fee, meaning that everyone in the community can join in.

Libraries are also important when it **(5)**_____ to preserving our cultural history. They collect, preserve and make available materials that document our history and culture. This includes books, manuscripts, photographs, maps and other materials that might otherwise **(6)**_____ lost.

Access to technology is of course provided **(7)**_____ libraries too, and it is true that many people might not otherwise have such access. This includes computers, internet access, and other digital resources that are essential for success in today's **(8)**_____.

1	**A** afford	**B** deliver	**C** lend	**D** provide
2	**A** of	**B** off	**C** for	**D** to
3	**A** giving	**B** taking	**C** offering	**D** passing
4	**A** tuition	**B** literature	**C** schooling	**D** literacy
5	**A** means	**B** comes	**C** happens	**D** arises
6	**A** be	**B** are	**C** were	**D** being
7	**A** by	**B** for	**C** in	**D** with
8	**A** earth	**B** world	**C** planet	**D** globe

Part 2

For questions 9–16, read the text below and decide which word best fits each gap. Use only one word for each gap. In the separate answer sheet, write your answers in capital letters, using one box per letter.

Freedman's Bank

The Freedman's Savings and Trust Company, also **(9)**_____ as Freedman's Bank, was established in 1865 in Washington D.C. It was the first African American-owned and operated bank in the United States.

The bank was established by the US government as a **(10)**_____ of the Civil War and the abolition of slavery. The bank's founder and first president was John W. Alvord, a white philanthropist and abolitionist who had long advocated **(11)**_____ economic opportunity for African Americans.

(12)_____ its noble intentions, however, the bank struggled from the start. It was underfunded and understaffed, and its leadership was often inexperienced and ineffective. Nonetheless, Freedman's Bank grew in popularity among African Americans, and, by the **(13)**_____ of the 1860s, just before 1870, it had more than 9,000 depositors, over $1 million in assets and branch offices throughout the South.

However, the bank's success was short-lived. In 1870, the bank's management was handed **(14)**_____ to a group of businessmen who were more interested in making a profit than in serving the needs of African Americans, ultimately leading to the bank's collapse in 1874. The demise of Freedman's Bank was devastating for many African American depositors, **(15)**_____ lost their life savings.

Freedman's Bank remains an important chapter in the history of African American finance. It was an early **(16)**_____ to provide economic opportunity to a marginalised community, and it served as a model for later efforts to establish black-owned banks and financial institutions.

Part 3

For questions 17–24, use the stem word on the right to form the correct word that fills each gap. In the separate answer sheet, write your answers in capital letters, using one box per letter.

Michael Jordan

Michael Jordan is widely regarded as one of the (17)_____ basketball players of all time. During his illustrious career, he won six NBA championships and five Most Valuable Player awards and played in the All-Star team 14 times. His (18)_____ and competitiveness were unmatched, and he (19)_____ the game of basketball with his signature moves such as 'the fadeaway jumper' and dunking from the free-throw line.

GREAT

ATHLETE
REVOLUTION

Jordan's impact on the sport of basketball cannot be (20)_____. His incredible skills on the court inspired a generation of young players and helped to popularise the sport around the world. He also set a high standard for excellence, both on and off the court, and his work ethic and (21)_____ to his craft continue to serve as an inspiration to athletes in all sports.

STATE

DEDICATE

Beyond his (22)_____ in basketball, Jordan's legacy extends to his business ventures and philanthropic efforts. He is the owner of the Charlotte Hornets NBA franchise, and his Jordan brand has become a global icon in the world of fashion and footwear. He is also known for his (23)_____ work, including his support of education and healthcare initiatives.

ACHIEVE

CHARITY

Overall, Michael Jordan's impact on sports and popular culture is (24)_____. He remains an enduring figure in the world of basketball, and his legacy as an athlete, entrepreneur and philanthropist continues to inspire millions around the world.

DENY

Part 4

For questions 25–30, complete the second sentence, using the word given, so that it has a similar meaning to the first sentence. Do not change the word provided and use between three and six words in total. In the separate answer sheet, write your answers in capital letters, using one box per letter.

25 Although Mila is short, she can play basketball rather well.

BEING

Despite _____ basketball rather well.

26 I didn't like Martha at first, it took me a while.

WARM

It took me a while _____ Martha at first.

27 Amit didn't go to the cinema because he had no money.

IF

Amit would have gone to the cinema _____.

28 She wondered if she would ever see him again.

WHETHER

She _____ ever see him again.

29 He was really happy with what he had produced.

PRIDE

He _____ what he had produced.

30 The rugby club is now being run by my friend's father.

TAKEN

My friend's father _____ the running of the rugby club.

**Answer sheet: Cambridge C1 Advanced
Use of English**

Test No.

Mark out of 36

Name _____ Date _____

Part 1: Multiple choice

8 marks

Mark the appropriate answer (A, B, C or D).

0	A	B	C	D

1	A	B	C	D		5	A	B	C	D
2	A	B	C	D		6	A	B	C	D
3	A	B	C	D		7	A	B	C	D
4	A	B	C	D		8	A	B	C	D

Part 2: Open cloze

8 marks

Write your answers in capital letters, using one box per letter.

0	B	E	C	A	U	S	E				

9											
10											
11											
12											
13											
14											
15											
16											

Part 3: Word formation

Write your answers in capital letters, using one box per letter.

17

18

19

20

21

22

23

24

Part 4: Key word transformation

Write your answers in capital letters, using one box per letter.

25

26

27

28

29

30

Cambridge
C1 Advanced
Use of English

Test 9

Part 1

For questions 1–8, read the text below and decide which answer best fits each gap. In the separate answer sheet, mark the appropriate answer (A, B, C or D).

Eurovision

Eurovision is an international song competition that has been **(1)**_____ annually since 1956. The contest is organised by the European Broadcasting Union and is one of the longest-running television programmes in the world. The competition has become an important cultural event in Europe, and in recent years it has gained a global **(2)**_____.

The origins of Eurovision can be **(3)**_____ back to the early 1950s when the European Broadcasting Union (EBU) was formed. The EBU aimed to promote cooperation between European broadcasters, and it was decided that a song competition would be an ideal **(4)**_____ to showcase the musical talent of each country. The first contest was held in 1956, with just seven countries **(5)**_____. Over the years, the competition has grown in popularity and now features acts from over 40 countries.

Eurovision has become an important event in the modern music industry. The competition provides a platform for aspiring musicians to showcase their talent on an international stage. Many famous musicians **(6)**_____ ABBA, Celine Dion and Julio Iglesias have **(7)**_____ their careers doing Eurovision.

In recent years, Eurovision has become a major cultural event, with millions of viewers tuning **(8)**_____ to watch the competition each year. The contest has also become a hotbed for political controversy, with some countries using the event as a platform to express political messages.

1	**A** placed	**B** held	**C** organised	**D** run
2	**A** following	**B** admiring	**C** watching	**D** supporting
3	**A** gone	**B** found	**C** discovered	**D** traced
4	**A** tactic	**B** way	**C** strategy	**D** state
5	**A** participating	**B** challenging	**C** undergoing	**D** playing
6	**A** entering	**B** bringing	**C** including	**D** involving
7	**A** activated	**B** originated	**C** launched	**D** increased
8	**A** over	**B** up	**C** out	**D** in

Part 2

For questions 9–16, read the text below and decide which word best fits each gap. Use only one word for each gap. In the separate answer sheet, write your answers in capital letters, using one box per letter.

Uplifting technology

The history of lifts, elevators and escalators dates back to ancient times when humans used pulleys and hoists to transport goods and people. However, it was not **(9)**_____ the 19th century that the modern passenger elevator was invented.

The first passenger elevator was **(10)**_____ by Elisha Otis in 1852. Otis created a safety brake that would prevent the elevator from falling **(11)**_____ the cable broke, which made **(12)**_____ possible for elevators to be used for safely transporting people. This then brought the construction of taller buildings and skyscrapers.

(13)_____ cities grew, the demand for faster and more efficient elevators increased, and, in the early 20th century, hydraulic and electric elevators were developed, **(14)**_____ made elevators faster and more reliable.

Escalators, on the other hand, appeared in the late 19th century by Jesse Reno. The first escalator was installed in Coney Island in 1896, and it quickly **(15)**_____ a popular attraction. It was in the early 20th century that escalators began to be installed in department stores and **(16)**_____ public buildings.

Today, lifts, elevators and escalators are essential parts of modern infrastructure. They are found in almost every tall building, airport and shopping mall, and in most public places.

Part 3

For questions 17–24, use the stem word on the right to form the correct word that fills each gap. In the separate answer sheet, write your answers in capital letters, using one box per letter.

The Santiago Bernabéu Stadium

The Santiago Bernabéu Stadium is home to the **(17)**_____ Real Madrid Football Club. The stadium, **ICON** which was inaugurated in 1947, has recently been completely refurbished to improve the overall experience for fans and players **(18)**_____. The project involved taking down **LIKE** and **(19)**_____ parts of the original stadium. The new **BUILD** design includes state-of-the-art technology, such as a retractable roof and a video screen that covers the stadium from all angles. These **(20)**_____ ensure that spectators **ADD** have an excellent view of the game, regardless of their location within the stadium. On top of this, new restaurants, bars and VIP areas have been added, providing visitors with a wider range of food and drink options to **(21)**_____ after an exciting **FUEL** game.

The **(22)**_____ of the Bernabéu Stadium has also had **RENOVATE** a positive impact on the community of Madrid, as the project created jobs and **(23)**_____ the local economy. The **BOOST** stadium is a popular tourist destination, and the improved facilities and services will likely increase the number of visitors to Madrid.

The Bernabéu Stadium is now ready to welcome football fans from all over the world and will **(24)**_____ continue to **HOPE** do so for years to come.

Part 4

For questions 25–30, complete the second sentence, using the word given, so that it has a similar meaning to the first sentence. Do not change the word provided and use between three and six words in total. In the separate answer sheet, write your answers in capital letters, using one box per letter.

25 The woman had a feeling that her neighbour was watching her.

WATCHED

The woman had a feeling that _____ by her neighbour.

26 This is the most boring match I have ever seen.

MORE

I have _____ match.

27 My brother hates it when people speak badly to him.

BEING

My brother hates _____ so badly.

28 She said that she would try and finish her homework.

BEST

She said that she would _____ finish her homework.

29 The weather has shown some improvement this afternoon.

SIGNS

The weather has _____ improving this afternoon.

30 If your mother didn't work all the time, you would have no money.

FOR

Were it not _____ all the time, you would have no money.

Test No.

Mark out of 36

Name _____   **Date** _____

Part 1: Multiple choice

8 marks

Mark the appropriate answer (A, B, C or D).

| 0 | A | B | C | D |

1	A	B	C	D		5	A	B	C	D
2	A	B	C	D		6	A	B	C	D
3	A	B	C	D		7	A	B	C	D
4	A	B	C	D		8	A	B	C	D

Part 2: Open cloze

8 marks

Write your answers in capital letters, using one box per letter.

| 0 | B | E | C | A | U | S | E | | | | |

9											
10											
11											
12											
13											
14											
15											
16											

Part 3: Word formation

Write your answers in capital letters, using one box per letter.

17

18

19

20

21

22

23

24

Part 4: Key word transformation

Write your answers in capital letters, using one box per letter.

25

26

27

28

29

30

Cambridge
C1 Advanced
Use of English

Test 10

Part 1

For questions 1–8, read the text below and decide which answer best fits each gap. In the separate answer sheet, mark the appropriate answer (A, B, C or D).

Are Eggs Good For You?

Eggs have been a **(1)**_____ of human diets for centuries and are considered one of the most versatile and nutrient-dense foods available. However, their reputation has been tarnished over the years **(2)**_____ to concerns about cholesterol levels and saturated fat content. So, the question remains: are eggs good for you?

On the one hand, eggs provide an excellent source of protein, **(3)**_____ vitamins and minerals such as vitamin D, vitamin B12 and selenium. They are also **(4)**_____ low in calories, making them an ideal food for weight loss and maintenance. Additionally, research has shown that eggs can help reduce the **(5)**_____ of heart disease and stroke, improve brain function and promote healthy eyesight.

On the other hand, one large egg contains around 186 milligrams of cholesterol, which is a significant amount for people with high cholesterol levels. Additionally, the yolk of an egg is high in saturated fat, which has been linked to an increased risk of heart disease.

While eggs are **(6)**_____ a nutrient-dense and healthy food, they may not be suitable for everyone. People with high cholesterol levels or a history of heart disease should consume eggs in moderation, and those who are vegan should seek alternative sources of protein. As with any food, balance and moderation are **(7)**_____, and it is essential to consider individual dietary needs and health concerns when **(8)**_____ dietary choices.

1	A	dominant	B	primary	C	staple	D	principal
2	A	due	B	because	C	since	D	as
3	A	requisite	B	essential	C	crucial	D	required
4	A	approximately	B	relatively	C	accordingly	D	adequately
5	A	hazard	B	danger	C	consequences	D	risk
6	A	positively	B	currently	C	undoubtedly	D	questionably
7	A	basic	B	key	C	main	D	significant
8	A	making	B	building	C	creating	D	reaching

Part 2

For questions 9–16, read the text below and decide which word best fits each gap. Use only one word for each gap. In the separate answer sheet, write your answers in capital letters, using one box per letter.

Vegemite and Marmite

Vegemite and Marmite are two popular food spreads made from yeast extract. They are both dark brown and **(9)**_____ a strong, salty flavour.

Vegemite is a spread that is popular in Australia and New Zealand. It is made from leftover brewer's yeast extract and is **(10)**_____ by-product of beer production. Vegemite is known for its salty and slightly bitter taste and is often spread on toast or used **(11)**_____ a seasoning in cooking.

Marmite is a similar spread that is popular in the United Kingdom and some **(12)**_____ parts of the world. Like Vegemite, it is made from yeast extract, but it has a slightly different taste. Marmite is also known for its salty and slightly bitter flavour, and it is often used as a spread on toast, a seasoning in cooking or paired **(13)**_____ cheese

While both spreads have a loyal fan base, they are **(14)**_____ interchangeable. Vegemite and Marmite have slightly different flavour profiles, and fans of **(15)**_____ may not necessarily enjoy the other. Additionally, the availability of the spreads can vary depending on the region, with Vegemite being **(16)**_____ commonly found in Australia and Marmite prevalent in the UK.

Part 3

For questions 17–24, use the stem word on the right to form the correct word that fills each gap. In the separate answer sheet, write your answers in capital letters, using one box per letter.

Times Tables Rock Stars

Times Tables Rock Stars is a popular academic app designed to help children improve their mathematical skills. Developed in the United Kingdom, the game allows children to choose their own avatar and compete against others in timed **(17)**_____ challenges. The platform is gamified, with different levels and challenges that allow children to progress as they improve their skills. **MULTIPLY**

The **(18)**_____ of Times Tables Rock Stars has grown exponentially in recent years, and it has **(19)**_____ a large following across the globe. The app's engaging format and **(20)**_____ nature make it a firm favourite amongst children, who are often eager to improve their scores and beat their friends.

POPULAR

GAIN

COMPETE

One of the reasons for its success is that it can be played on a variety of devices, making it easy for children to practise wherever they are. The user-friendly **(21)**_____ also makes it easy for children to navigate, **(22)**_____ them to focus on their learning and progress without being held up by **(23)**_____ controls or menu options.

FACE

ALLOW

CONFUSE

The app is admired all over the world which is a testament to its **(24)**_____ design, and it is likely that its success will continue to grow for years to come. **INNOVATION**

Part 4

For questions 25–30, complete the second sentence, using the word given, so that it has a similar meaning to the first sentence. **Do not change the word provided and use between three and six words in total.** In the separate answer sheet, write your answers in capital letters, using one box per letter.

25 The manager was considering hiring a new person for the office.

THOUGHT

The manager _____ a new person for the office.

26 My friend said that Janice will arrive later this evening.

EXPECTED

My friend said that Janice _____ later this evening.

27 Michael hasn't seen his family for years.

SINCE

It's been _____ his family.

28 Max said that he had always intended to invite Mitchell to the party.

MY

"It had _____ to invite Mitchell to the party," said Max.

29 You might get thirsty on the way there so take a bottle of water with you.

CASE

Take a bottle of water with you _____ on the way there.

30 What did she wear at the party?

WAS

What _____ at the party?

Mark out of 36

Name _____ **Date** _____

Part 1: Multiple choice

8 marks

Mark the appropriate answer (A, B, C or D).

0	A	B	C	D

1	A	B	C	D		5	A	B	C	D
2	A	B	C	D		6	A	B	C	D
3	A	B	C	D		7	A	B	C	D
4	A	B	C	D		8	A	B	C	D

Part 2: Open cloze

8 marks

Write your answers in capital letters, using one box per letter.

0	B	E	C	A	U	S	E				

9											
10											
11											
12											
13											
14											
15											
16											

Part 3: Word formation

Write your answers in capital letters, using one box per letter.

17

18

19

20

21

22

23

24

Part 4: Key word transformation

Write your answers in capital letters, using one box per letter.

25

26

27

28

29

30

Answers

Test 1

Part 1: Multiple choice						
1	B	facing	5	B	down
2	D	traffic	6	C	impact
3	A	strain	7	B	calls
4	A	address	8	A	through

Part 2: Open cloze			
9	on	13	also
10	lead	14	This
11	out	15	the
12	be	16	step

Part 3: Word formation			
17	strategic	21	ability
18	renewable	22	building
19	further	23	careful
20	consumption	24	functional

Part 4: Key word transformation		
	Lexical	*Grammatical*
25	be	of (any) assistance
26	a matter	of time
27	On	no account
28	has (been)	turned into
29	on	good terms
30	pulling	out by

Test 2

Part 1: Multiple choice						
1	**B**	structure	**5**	**C**	home
2	**A**	works	**6**	**D**	of
3	**B**	responsible	**7**	**A**	notable
4	**D**	ambitious	**8**	**C**	captivate

Part 2: Open cloze			
9	up	**13**	past
10	have	**14**	breath
11	By	**15**	ones
12	mean	**16**	every / the / each

Part 3: Word formation			
17	characteristics	**21**	primarily
18	length	**22**	conservation
19	distinction	**23**	endangered
20	behaviourally	**24**	better

Part 4: Key word transformation		
	Lexical	*Grammatical*
25	before	have I had
26	ineffective	at / in stopping
27		of being cancelled
28	in	danger of
29	in	a request for
30	get	to the point

Test 3

Part 1: Multiple choice						
1	**A**	evolved	**5**	**B**	rise	
2	**B**	innovative	**6**	**C**	streamlined	
3	**B**	revolution	**7**	**D**	apprehensive	
4	**A**	store	**8**	**B**	barriers	

Part 2: Open cloze			
9	over	**13**	of
10	two	**14**	for
11	height	**15**	close
12	out	**16**	all / those

Part 3: Word formation			
17	thinning	**21**	acceptance
18	genetic	**22**	popularised
19	specific	**23**	well-being
20	disorders	**24**	advantageous

Part 4: Key word transformation		
	Lexical	*Grammatical*
25	no	less than
26	out	much hope
27	put	at risk
28	led	you to believe
29	to	have forgotten
30	just	as much

Test 4

Part 1: Multiple choice						
1	C	revered		5	C	Throughout
2	D	legend		6	A	sight
3	A	process		7	B	surrounded
4	D	well		8	B	steeped

Part 2: Open cloze			
9	have	13	all
10	of	14	living
11	breaks	15	aside
12	cost	16	such

Part 3: Word formation			
17	interface	21	widening
18	cultural	22	controversy
19	led	23	misinformation
20	ability	24	widespread

Part 4: Key word transformation		
	Lexical	*Grammatical*
25	dream(s)	come true
26	will	have been married
27	despite	the company offering
28	are required	to speak for
29	lost	track of
30	not	as interesting as

Test 5

Part 1: Multiple choice						
1	D	progressive	5	D	replenish
2	B	thought	6	B	cure
3	A	role	7	A	mimic
4	D	undergone	8	B	While

Part 2: Open cloze			
9	through	13	to
10	once	14	now
11	peace	15	or
12	in	16	fall

Part 3: Word formation			
17	dramatically	21	lose
18	correspondence	22	forcing
19	deeper	23	inconvenient
20	drawbacks	24	limitations

Part 4: Key word transformation		
	Lexical	**Grammatical**
25	every	Intention of
26	to	figure out (a solution to)
27	get	round to fixing
28	was	being driven
29	if	she was staying
30	insist	on moving

Test 6

Part 1: Multiple choice						
1	**C**	tips	**5**	**A**	layer
2	**B**	vulnerabilities	**6**	**B**	protect
3	**C**	giving	**7**	**B**	them
4	**A**	alert	**8**	**D**	victim

Part 2: Open cloze			
9	were	**13**	a
10	not	**14**	way
11	to	**15**	touch
12	still	**16**	more

Part 3: Word formation			
17	addition	**21**	fitting
18	diversity	**22**	refreshing
19	reflected	**23**	deeper
20	narrative	**24**	relatable

Part 4: Key word transformation		
	Lexical	*Grammatical*
25	had	our photograph taken
26	may	have come round
27	keep	it to
28	tried	her best
29	were	you able
30	fell	through

Test 7

Part 1: Multiple choice						
1	**B**	popularity	**5**	**C**	even
2	**B**	which	**6**	**B**	means
3	**A**	praised	**7**	**C**	job
4	**D**	compelling	**8**	**A**	stay

Part 2: Open cloze			
9	It	**13**	back
10	located	**14**	until
11	on	**15**	its
12	as	**16**	part

Part 3: Word formation			
17	renowned	**21**	adaptation
18	degradation	**22**	strengths
19	remarkable	**23**	analysis
20	effectively	**24**	biodiversity

Part 4: Key word transformation		
	Lexical	*Grammatical*
25	this	time last
26	not	like him
27	it	got the harder
28	put	up with his behaviour
29	was	wondering if
30	make	a/any difference

Test 8

Part 1: Multiple choice

1	D	provide	5	B	comes
2	A	of	6	A	be
3	C	offering	7	A	by
4	D	a	8	B	world

Part 2: Open cloze

9	known	13	end
10	result	14	over
11	for	15	who
12	despite	16	attempt

Part 3: Word formation

17	greatest	21	dedication
18	athleticism	22	achievements
19	revolutionised	23	charitable
20	overstated	24	undeniable

Part 4: Key word transformation

	Lexical	*Grammatical*
25	being	short Mila can play
26	to	warm to
27	if	he had had (any)money
28	wondered	whether she would
29	took	pride in
30	has	taken over

Test 9

Part 1: Multiple choice						
1	**B**	held	**5**	**A**	participating
2	**A**	following	**6**	**C**	including
3	**D**	traced	**7**	**C**	launched
4	**B**	way	**8**	**D**	in

Part 2: Open cloze			
9	until	**13**	As
10	invented	**14**	which
11	if	**15**	became
12	it	**16**	other / many

Part 3: Word formation			
17	iconic	**21**	refuel
18	alike	**22**	renovation
19	rebuilding	**23**	boosted
20	additions	**24**	hopefully

Part 4: Key word transformation		
	Lexical	*Grammatical*
25	she	was being watched
26	never	seen a more boring
27		being spoken to
28	try	her best to
29	shown	(some) signs of
30	for	your mother working

Test 10

Part 1: Multiple choice						
1	**C**	staple	**5**	**D**	risk
2	**A**	due	**6**	**C**	undoubtedly
3	**B**	essential	**7**	**B**	key
4	**B**	relatively	**8**	**A**	making

Part 2: Open cloze			
9	have	**13**	with
10	a	**14**	not
11	as / for	**15**	one
12	other	**16**	more

Part 3: Word formation			
17	multiplication	**21**	interface
18	popularity	**22**	allowing
19	gained	**23**	confusing
20	competitive	**24**	innovative

Part 4: Key word transformation		
	Lexical	*Grammatical*
25	(had)	thought about hiring
26	is	expected to arrive
27		years since Michael saw / has seen
28	always	been my intention
29		in case you get thirsty
30	was	she wearing

Printed in the USA
CPSIA information can be obtained
at www.ICGtesting.com
LVHW062350250823
756187LV00015B/682